Project Management

Practical Tools for Success

Third Edition

Marion E. Haynes

A Fifty-Minute™ Series Book

This Fifty-Minute™ book is designed to be "read with a pencil." It is an excellent workbook for self-study as well as classroom learning. All material is copyright-protected and cannot be duplicated without permission from the publisher. *Therefore, be sure to order a copy for every training participant by contacting:*

CRISP.
Learning
Menlo Park, California

1-800-442-7477

CrispLearning.com

Project Management

Practical Tools for Success

Third Edition

Marion E. Haynes

CREDITS:
Senior Editor: **Debbie Woodbury**
Editor: **Brenda Pittsley**
Assistant Editor: **Genevieve Del Rosario**
Production Manager: **Judy Petry**
Design: **Nicole Phillips**
Production Artist: **Zach Hooker**
Cartoonist: **Ralph Mapson**

© 1989, 1996, 2002 Crisp Publications, Inc.
Printed in the United States of America by Von Hoffmann Graphics, Inc.

CrispLearning.com

658.404
Hayn

02 03 04 05   10 9 8 7 6 5 4 3 2

Library of Congress Catalog Card Number 2001096811
Haynes, Marion E.
Project Management
ISBN 1-56052-665-3

Learning Objectives For:

PROJECT MANAGEMENT

The objectives for *Project Management* are listed below. They have been developed to guide you, the reader, to the core issues covered in this book.

THE OBJECTIVES OF THIS BOOK ARE:

❑ 1) To present the basic principles of project management

❑ 2) To explain the tools of project management

❑ 3) To discuss the role of the project manager

ASSESSING YOUR PROGRESS

In addition to the learning objectives, Crisp Learning has developed an **assessment** that covers the fundamental information presented in this book. A 25-item, multiple-choice and true-false questionnaire allows the reader to evaluate his or her comprehension of the subject matter. To learn how to obtain a copy of this assessment, please call **1-800-442-7477** and ask to speak with a Customer Service Representative.

Assessments should not be used in any employee selection process.

About the Author

Marion E. Haynes is an adult educator specializing in management and supervisory training. He began his career in employee relations with a major oil company in 1956 and retired in 1991. He has published more than thirty articles in professional and trade journals, and nine other books on planning and management skills. He has presented management training workshops under the sponsorship of several universities in the south-central states and has been the featured speaker at many trade and professional association gatherings.

Marion Haynes holds an M.B.A. with distinction in management from New York University. He has specialized in the design, presentation, and evaluation of management training since 1968.

How to Use This Book

This *Fifty-Minute™ Series Book* is a unique, user-friendly product. As you read through the material, you will quickly experience the interactive nature of the book. There are numerous exercises, real-world case studies, and examples that invite your opinion, as well as checklists, tips, and concise summaries that reinforce your understanding of the concepts presented.

A Crisp Learning *Fifty-Minute™ Book* can be used in variety of ways. Individual self-study is one of the most common. However, many organizations use *Fifty-Minute* books for pre-study before a classroom training session. Other organizations use the books as a part of a systemwide learning program—supported by video and other media based on the content in the books. Still others work with Crisp Learning to customize the material to meet their specific needs and reflect their culture. Regardless of how it is used, we hope you will join the more than 20 million satisfied learners worldwide who have completed a *Fifty-Minute Book*.

Preface

Everyone manages projects from time to time. For example, students manage a project fulfilling class requirements. The do-it-yourselfer manages a project fixing or building something around the house. A host manages a social event. These people can capitalize on the same concepts of project management as those used by engineers, superintendents, and contractors.

Project Management is written to help you carry out your projects successfully. The lessons do not presume any prior knowledge of managerial or technical subjects. Successful management of any project depends not only on careful scheduling, adequate resources, and continual measurement, it also requires ongoing and clear communication. This third edition contains new emphasis on the importance of ensuring understanding through good listening skills.

Questionnaires, checklists, and exercises are used throughout the book to emphasize the material presented. Work through these elements as you go along. They will reinforce the concepts you are learning. Successful project management is within your grasp. Simply read, understand, and apply the ideas contained in this book.

Good Luck!

Marion E. Haynes
Springdale, Arkansas

Contents

Part 1: Introduction

Part 2: Defining the Project

Part 3: Planning the Project

Part 4: Implementing the Plan

Part 5: Completing the Project

Part 6: Summary

Introduction

What Is Project Management?

Project management focuses on a project. A project is an undertaking that has a beginning and an end, and is carried out to meet established goals within cost, schedule, and quality objectives.

Project management brings together and optimizes the resources necessary to successfully complete the project. These resources include the skills, talents, and cooperative efforts of a team of people; facilities, tools, and equipment; information, systems, and techniques; and money.

How Did Project Management Develop?

The concept of project management as a discipline was developed to manage the U.S. space program in the early 1960s. Its practice expanded rapidly into government, the military, and industry. Today you will find its principles applied to program management, product management, and construction management.

How Does Project Management Differ from Other Management Principles?

Project management differs in two significant ways. First, while department managers or managers of other organizational units expect their departments to exist indefinitely, project managers focus on an undertaking with a finite life span. Second, projects frequently need resources on a temporary basis, whereas permanent organizations try to utilize resources full-time. The sharing of resources frequently leads to conflict and requires skillful negotiation to see that projects get the necessary resources to meet objectives throughout the life cycle of a project.

The Project Life Cycle

Each project moves through a predictable life cycle of four phases, with each phase calling for different skills from the project manager. The phases of a project life cycle are:

> **Conceiving and defining the project**

> **Planning the project**

> **Implementing the plan**

> **Completing and evaluating the project**

Each phase is discussed in this book.

Typical Activity Levels During the Phases of a Project's Life

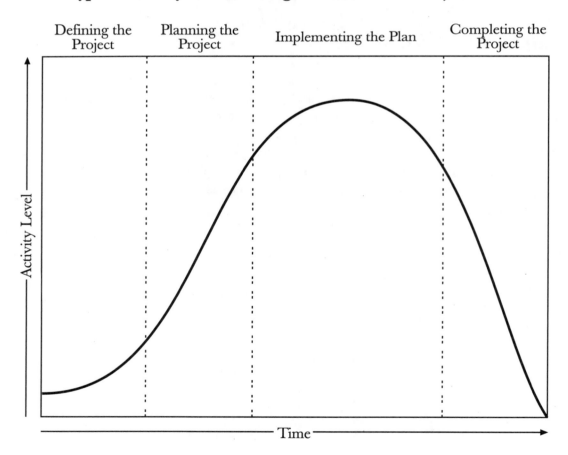

Defining the Project   Planning the Project   Implementing the Plan   Completing the Project

Activity Level

Time

YOUR PROJECT MANAGEMENT EXPERIENCE

Think of a project you have completed within the last two or three months. It may have been a weekend project at home or something at work.

Now, respond to the following questions:

1. When did you first get the idea for the project? How much time elapsed and what steps were involved between the idea conception and a clear understanding of what you were going to do?

_____

_____

_____

_____

_____

_____

_____

2. How did you go about planning the project? Did you think about what tools, equipment, and supplies you would need, and where to obtain them? Did you arrange for extra help if you could not handle the project alone?

_____

_____

_____

_____

_____

_____

_____

CONTINUED

3. Once you got under way, did everything go according to plan? Did you stay within budget? Did you finish on time? Did you meet your quality standards? Did any unanticipated problems occur? If so, how did you deal with them?

_____

_____

_____

_____

_____

4. When the project was completed, were there people to be released or reassigned, tools and equipment to be returned, or surplus material to be disposed of?

_____

_____

_____

_____

_____

5. After the project was completed, did you spend any time reflecting on the experience to see where improvements could have been made in the management of the project? If not, take a few minutes now and write down some ideas for improvement.

_____

_____

_____

_____

_____

Project Parameters

During a project's life, management of it focuses on three basic parameters:

- ➤ **Quality**

- ➤ **Time**

- ➤ **Cost**

A successfully managed project is one that is completed at the specified level of quality, on or before the deadline, and within budget.

Each of these parameters should be specified in detail during the planning phase of the project. These specifications then form the basis for control during the implementation phase.

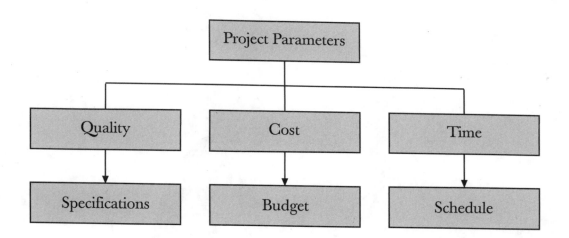

Negotiating Specifications with the Client

If there is a client involved who must accept the project upon completion, the specifications that define a successful outcome must be negotiated and agreed to by the client, and included as part of the contract.

A client may be either internal or external. Also, there may be more than one "client," especially when the project is internal to a company. For example, the case study used throughout this book is a project to construct more workspace within a company. The clients are the department that will use the space, and management, both of whom must agree to the budget and schedule.

In the course of a project, specifications may change. The project manager has a responsibility to make sure the client—whether external or internal—agrees to the revised specifications. If there is a written contract, it needs to be adjusted and all involved parties must sign off on it. This ensures that the project team and the client will be in agreement on the acceptable parameters of success when the final inspection is done.

A Word About Communicating

Communication skills permeate the entire process of project management. Successful project managers communicate effectively with their clients, team members, and those upon whom they depend for goods and services. As a project manager, you must share information, establish clear expectations, and build a group of people into a smooth functioning team.

Effective communication in face-to-face settings, on the telephone, and by e-mail is inherent to the skillful use of delegation, feedback, and negotiation. Each of these ideas will be addressed at various points in this book, but it is not too soon to mention the importance of the most basic communication skill—listening. Your success, and the success of the project, will depend on your ability to listen—and hear—what is being said, as well what is *not* being said, by all participants.

Listening Skills

It is just as important for you to understand what others are telling you as it is for you to be understood. But this is no easy task. Hearing is not listening. Listening is not understanding. Listening depends on hearing and leads to understanding. It is the process of taking in information and synthesizing it into something that is understood.

Understanding grows from good listening. What someone doesn't say, or avoids saying, often is more important to full understanding than what is said. To be a fully effective listener, you must be both physically and intellectually engaged in the process.

The activity on the following page will help you assess your listening skills. Complete it carefully and honestly; the results will help you determine where you should focus your energies to improve your communication skills and achieve better results with your project team.

ASSESS YOUR LISTENING SKILLS

Place a check next to the statements you believe you have mastered.

- ❏ When someone asks me something that I don't fully understand, I ask for clarification.
- ❏ I typically pay close attention when talking with someone.
- ❏ I listen for meaning, rather than just words.
- ❏ I never pretend to listen when I'm not.
- ❏ I'm careful to distinguish between inference and fact.
- ❏ I don't allow my feelings about a subject to interfere with hearing what someone has to say.
- ❏ I don't let emotion-laden words arouse antagonism.
- ❏ I don't tune people out because the subject they're talking about is not interesting to me.
- ❏ I try to identify my purpose for listening to someone.
- ❏ I don't listen primarily for facts.
- ❏ I listen for what's being left out.
- ❏ I maintain comfortable eye contact with the person I'm talking with.
- ❏ I'm relaxed but attentive during discussions.
- ❏ I listen to how something is said as well as to what is said.
- ❏ I pay attention to non-verbal behavior.
- ❏ I check for understanding of what is said rather than assume I understand.
- ❏ I avoid making absolute statements.

How can you improve as a listener? _____

_____

_____

Tips for Becoming a Better Communicator

➤ Pay attention when someone talks to you. Focus your attention and energy on listening.

➤ Maintain eye contact during discussions.

➤ Concentrate on what is said. Don't be distracted by appearance, style, or mannerisms.

➤ Verify your understanding of what you're told through questions and summaries.

➤ Avoid slang, jargon, and acronyms unless you know they will be understood.

➤ Check your understanding of what you see rather than assuming or drawing incorrect inferences.

➤ Maintain a tentativeness in your conclusions rather than taking a dogmatic position.

➤ Be cautious about blaming or judging others. Check your facts and state your position, then examine any differences in perception.

➤ When something goes wrong, treat it as an opportunity to improve in the future rather than expending energy identifying who is at fault.

➤ Use "I" statements to describe how you see things rather than "you" statements, which can seem judgmental and threatening.

➤ Use indefinite pronouns carefully. You communicate much more clearly when you refer to someone or something by name rather than by "he," "she," or "it."

➤ Stay with a topic long enough to develop full understanding rather than flitting from topic to topic.

➤ Be willing to set your topic aside until the other person's has been discussed. Then return to yours.

➤ Use broad questions to open discussions and gain information. For example, you might ask, "How are things going?" rather than, "Have you finished that report yet?"

RATE YOURSELF AS A PROJECT MANAGER

Rate yourself on each of the following skills required to be a successful project manager. Place a check (✔) next to the skill you feel confident about. When you're finished, those that are not checked represent opportunities for development.

My current project management skills include:

❏ Organizing a project from beginning to end.

❏ Structuring a plan that will stand up under pressure.

❏ Getting people to accept my plan and support it.

❏ Setting measurable project objectives.

❏ Motivating team members.

❏ Helping team members solve problems.

❏ Utilizing available resources.

❏ Eliminating waste of time and money.

❏ Measuring project performance.

❏ Using information systems that respond to project needs.

❏ Communicating with everyone involved in the project.

❏ Listening to what others have to say.

Defining the Project

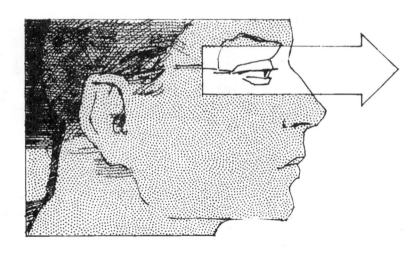

14

The Origin of Projects

Projects grow out of problems or opportunities. At work, they are initiated by upper management, clients, or staff members. At school, they may be initiated by teachers, students, or administrators; at home, by yourself or other family members. A project is born when someone reacts to the level of frustration surrounding a problem or someone sees an opportunity to move into a new venture. When a decision is made to do something about the problem or opportunity, a project is born—at this point someone is typically given the responsibility of carrying it out. That person becomes the project manager.

What Are the Pitfalls and How Can They Be Avoided?

A project's initiator is almost always unclear about important aspects of the project. Project personnel tend to stress their own points of view during the stage of defining and structuring the project. But disaster can result if personal biases and interests are left unchecked. Such disasters can be avoided by full discussion among the project manager, client, and staff at the project's inception. With a clear understanding of what is expected, the project manager is now ready to begin defining the project.

Getting Under Way: Action Items

When the nuclear project team is assembled, the first order of business is to clarify the project's definition and scope, as well as the basic strategy for carrying it out. The following sequence of action items will get your project smoothly under way.

    1. Study, discuss, and analyze.

    2. Write a project definition.

    3. Set an end-results objective.

    4. List imperatives and desirables.

    5. Generate alternative strategies.

    6. Evaluate alternatives.

    7. Choose a course of action.

Let's look at these steps in more depth.

1 Study, discuss, and analyze.

It is critical for the team to spend adequate time studying, discussing, and analyzing the project at the beginning. This establishes a clear understanding of what you are dealing with. It may be necessary to research how other teams structured their projects or what past experience can contribute to your project planning. The purpose of this activity is to be sure you are addressing the right problem or pursuing the real opportunity.

2 Write a project definition.

When you are confident that you have a firm grasp of the situation, work up a preliminary project definition. This preliminary definition will be subject to revision as additional information and experience is acquired.

3 Set an end-results objective.

Using the project definition, state the end-results objective to be met at the project's conclusion. (Guidelines follow on page 18.)

4 List imperatives and desirables.

Now list both the imperatives and desirables that will be part of the end results at the project's conclusion. That is, list the outcomes that must be present for the project to be considered successful, then list the outcomes that are nonessential but which would add to the project's success.

5 Generate alternative strategies.

Now you are ready to generate alternative strategies that might lead you to your objective. To generate these alternatives, try brainstorming with your project team (see technique on page 19).

6 Evaluate alternatives.

Next, evaluate the alternative strategies you have generated. Be sure that your criteria for evaluation are realistic and reflect the end-results objective.

7 Choose a course of action.

Evaluation allows you to choose a course of action that will meet both your project definition and end-results objectives.

Good Objectives Are SMART

In fulfilling the third action item—setting an end-results objective—it is important to know the elements that make up a good objective. The SMART acronym will help you craft your objective. Remember that a SMART objective is:

S **pecific.** A good objective says exactly what you want to accomplish.

M **easurable.** Being specific helps make your objective measurable.

A **ction-Oriented.** When writing objectives, use statements that have active verbs and are complete sentences.

R **ealistic.** Good objectives must be attainable yet present a challenge.

T **ime-limited.** Set a specific time by which to achieve the objective.

Example: *Complete landscaping by May 31, at a cost not to exceed $2,500.00.*

Write an objective for the same project you used to complete the exercise in Part 1:

_____

_____

_____

_____

_____

Brainstorming to Generate Alternatives

Brainstorming is a free-form process that taps the creative potential of a group through association of ideas. Association works as a two-way current: When a group member voices an idea, this stimulates ideas from others, which in turn lead to more ideas from the one who initiated the idea.

Brainstorming Guidelines

➤ List all ideas offered by group members.

➤ Do not evaluate or judge ideas at this time, or discuss ideas except to clarify understanding.

➤ Welcome "blue sky" ideas. It's easier to eliminate ideas later.

➤ Repetition is okay. Don't waste time sorting out duplication.

➤ Encourage quantity. The more ideas you generate, the greater your chance of finding a useful one.

BRAINSTORM

"Blue Sky" Ideas

Testing Your Preliminary Strategy

Before moving to a full-scale project, a feasibility study should be carried out to test your preliminary strategy and answer the basic question "Will it work?" Depending on the nature of the project, one or more of three methods will help answer this question. The choices are to do a *market study, pilot test,* or *computer simulation.*

The amount of money and other resources that are invested in feasibility studies must be in proportion to the amount of money that the project will put at risk. For example, a company that is planning to invest $450 million to retool a factory to manufacture a new appliance will probably consider a $250,000 market study an excellent investment if it clarifies the design of the appliance before the major investment is made. On the other hand, a franchised cookie company that is planning to add a new kind of cookie to its line can simply mix up a batch at one store, sell them for a week, and look at sales results—all for a modest investment in local advertising and special ingredients.

Market Study

If your project is to bring a new product to market, you must determine its market potential. Market research asks customers whether your product satisfies their current or potential perceived needs. You can also examine similar products to determine how your product is differentiated from those that are currently available.

Pilot Test

A pilot test is a small-scale tryout of your project. It could be a limited-area market test of a product or a working model of a construction project. Sometimes referred to as "field testing," a pilot test gives you the opportunity to observe your project's performance under actual conditions.

Computer Simulation

Many types of projects can be modeled on computers. For example, the market potential of a product can be predicted by analyzing demographic data of the target users along with certain assumptions about current and potential needs. The load-bearing potential of buildings, bridges, and vessels are analyzed through mathematical calculations.

Computer simulation is used in such diverse fields as aerodynamics, thermodynamics, optical design, and mechanical design. In some cases, the computer is used to assist with the actual design of the project. The major purpose of simulation is to identify potential problems before the project is under way.

Using the Study Results

If the results of a well-conceived and executed feasibility study indicate that the project should proceed, you can move confidently into detailed planning and implementation. If the results are discouraging, the data should be used to do a project redesign, followed by another feasibility study, and so on until a successful project concept is identified.

Progress Review: Parts 1 and 2

Write **T** for True or **F** for False in response to each of the following statements.

1. __ A project is an ongoing venture or activity.

2. __ Projects are initiated by whoever is in charge.

3. __ Communication is an important part of project management.

4. __ The project manager is responsible for carrying out the project.

5. __ Quality is not important in projects.

6. __ The project's initiator usually has a clear idea of all the important aspects of the project.

7. __ Completing a project on time is an important parameter of project management.

8. __ The project team needs to spend time clearly defining the project before getting under way.

9. __ Brainstorming has nothing to offer project management.

10. __ Completing a project within budget is not important.

11. __ Your basic strategy for completing a project should be tested before moving ahead.

12. __ A pilot test can be used to evaluate your strategy.

13. __ Computer simulation can help determine the feasibility of construction projects.

14. __ Project management is no different than any other application of management principles.

15. __ The temporary nature of projects leads to unique challenges for project managers.

Score Your Responses

1.	F	4.	T	7.	T	10.	F	13.	T
2.	F	5.	F	8.	T	11.	T	14.	F
3.	T	6.	T	9.	F	12.	T	15.	T

12 to 15 Excellent: You're ready to move on.

9 to 11 Good: A quick review would be helpful before you proceed.

0 to 8 Poor: You must have dozed off. Reread Parts 1 and 2.

Planning the Project

Planning the Three Project Parameters

Planning is crucial in project management. Planning means detailing what is required to successfully complete the project along the three critical dimensions:

- ➤ **Quality**

- ➤ **Time**

- ➤ **Cost**

Each of these dimensions will be considered in the following pages, along with a variety of tools and techniques for tracking them and ensuring that associated goals are met.

Planning Steps

- ❑ Establish the project objective.

- ❑ Choose a basic strategy for achieving the objective.

- ❑ Breakdown the project into logical steps or subunits.

- ❑ Determine the performance standards for each step.

- ❑ Determine how much time is required to complete each step.

- ❑ Determine the proper sequence for completing the steps or subunits and aggregate this information into a schedule for the total project.

- ❑ Determine the cost of each step and aggregate costs into the project budget.

- ❑ Design the necessary staff organization, including the number and kind of positions, and the duties and responsibilities of each.

- ❑ Determine what training, if any, is needed for project team members.

- ❑ Develop the necessary policies and procedures.

Planning the Quality Dimension

Planning for quality requires attention to detail. The goal of quality planning is to assure that the output of the finished project will do what it is supposed to do. A quality plan also establishes the criteria by which the project output will be evaluated when the project is finished.

In planning the qualitative dimension, include specifications for the quality and types of materials to be used, the performance standards to be met, and the means of verifying quality, such as testing and inspection. Two techniques—a work breakdown structure and project specifications—facilitate planning for quality. Both are described on the next few pages.

Creating a Work Breakdown Structure

A work breakdown structure (WBS) is the starting place for planning all three project parameters: quality, cost, and time. It is a technique based on dividing a project into steps, or units of work to be completed in a sequence. Because all elements required to complete the project are identified, a work breakdown structure reduces the chances of neglecting or overlooking an essential step.

A work breakdown structure is typically configured with two or three levels of detail, although more levels may be required for very complex projects. Start by identifying logical subdivisions of the project, and then break each of these down, thereby adding the second level. As you construct a work breakdown structure, keep in mind that the goal is to identify distinct units of work that will advance the project toward its completion.

CASE STUDY: Remodeling Project

Project: Remodel Building 7 to add four new offices by the end of the third quarter at a cost not to exceed $40,000.

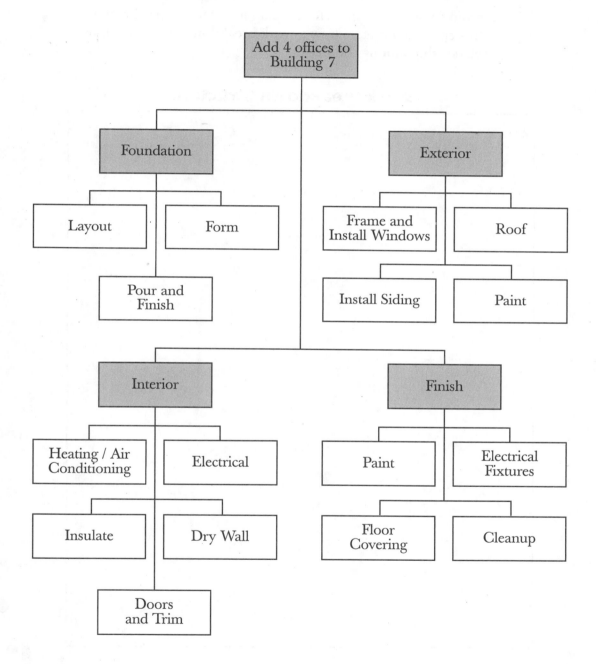

Practice Making a Work Breakdown Structure

Select a project you have completed or plan to complete and break it down into steps or subunits. Draw a work breakdown structure showing the relationship among the steps.

Work Breakdown Structure

Project Specifications

From the work breakdown structure, specifications can be written for each step of the project. Specifications include everything that is necessary to meet the project's quality dimension, including materials to be used, standards to be met, tests to be performed, and so on. Use extreme care in writing specifications, because they become the controlling factor in meeting project performance standards. They also directly affect both budget and schedule.

Example of Project Specifications:

Foundation

➤ Pour 4-inch concrete slab over 6 inches of compacted sand fill. Reinforce with 6-by-6-inch, No. 6 wire mash. Install 6 mil polyethylene membrane waterproofing barrier between sand and concrete.

➤ Use 1-foot-wide-by-1-foot-long-by-6-inch-deep beams around perimeter of foundation and under load-bearing walls, per blueprints. Beams to include No. 5 reinforcing steel bars in each corner positioned with three stirrups on 2-feet-by-6-inch centers.

➤ Concrete to withstand 2500 psi test after 28 days.

Now take the project for which you made a work breakdown structure and write specifications for at least one step of the project:

_____

_____

_____

_____

_____

_____

_____

_____

_____

Planning the Time Dimension

The objective when planning the time dimension is to determine the shortest time necessary to complete the project. Begin with the work breakdown structure and determine the time necessary to complete each step or subunit. Next, determine in what sequence the steps must be completed, and what steps can be under way simultaneously. From this analysis, you will determine the three most significant time elements:

➤ The duration of each step

➤ The earliest time at which a step may be started

➤ The latest time by which a step must be started

Planning the time dimension can be done only by people who have experience with the activities designated for each step. If you personally do not know how long it takes to do something, you will need to rely on someone who does have the requisite experience.

Many project managers find it realistic to estimate time intervals as a range rather than as a precise amount. Another way to deal with the lack of precision in estimating time is to use a commonly accepted formula for a task. If you are working with a mathematical model, you can determine the probability of the work being completed within the estimated time by calculating a standard deviation of the time estimate.

Using a Mathematical Model to Estimate Time

T_m–The most probable amount of time necessary to complete the project.

T_o–The optimistic (shortest) time, within which only 1% of similar projects are completed.

T_p–The pessimistic (longest) time, within which 99% of similar projects are completed.

T_e–The calculated time estimate.

$$T_e = \frac{T_o + 4T_m + T_p}{6}$$

$\sigma =$ Standard deviation

$$\sigma = \frac{T_p - T_o}{6}$$

The work will be completed within the range of $T_e \pm 1$ standard deviation 68.26% of the time.

The work will be completed within the range of $T_e \pm 2$ standard deviations 95.44% of the time.

The work will be completed within the range of $T_e \pm 3$ standard deviations 99.73% of the time.

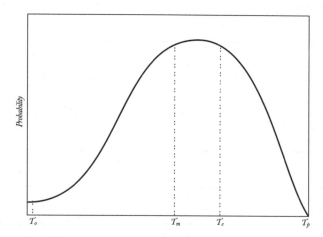

With a duration set for each subunit, the next step is to determine the earliest and latest times for starting each one. Gantt charts and PERT diagrams are two methods commonly used to chart a project. Both are discussed on the following pages.

PRACTICE ESTIMATING TIME

Using the same project that you have been using, determine a time estimate for each of the project's subunits or steps.

Subunit or Step	T_o	T_p	T_m	T_e

Gantt Chart

A Gantt chart is a horizontal bar graph that displays the time relationship of steps in a project. It is named after Henry Gantt, the industrial engineer who introduced the procedure in the early 1900s. Each step of a project is represented by a line placed on a chart in the time period it is to be undertaken. When completed, a Gantt chart shows a sequential flow of activities, as well as activities that can be under way at the same time.

To create a Gantt chart:

1. First list the steps required to complete a project and estimate the time required for each step.

2. Next, organize the steps down the left side of the chart and place the time intervals along the bottom.

3. Now draw a horizontal line next to each step, starting at the planned beginning date for the step and ending on its completion date.

Some parallel steps can be carried out at the same time even when one takes longer than the other. This allows some flexibility on when to start the shorter step; the start time is movable as long as the step is finished in time to flow into subsequent steps. This situation can be shown with a dotted line denoting potential slack time drawn out to the time when the step must be completed.

When your Gantt chart is finished, you will be able to see the minimum total time for the project, the proper sequence of steps, and which steps can be underway at the same time.

Example of a Gantt Chart

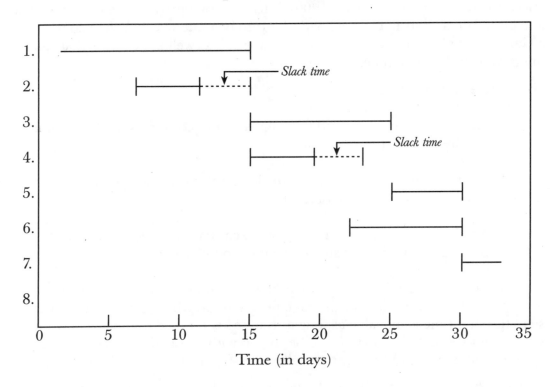

Time (in days)

Benefits

You can add to the usefulness of a Gantt chart by also charting actual progress. This is usually done by drawing a line in a different color below the original line to show the actual start and finish dates for each step. This allows you to quickly assess whether or not the project is on schedule.

Drawbacks

Gantt charts are limited in their ability to show the interdependencies of activities. In projects where the steps flow in a simple sequence of events, Gantt charts can portray adequate information for project management. However, when several steps are under way at the same time and a high level of interdependency exists among the various steps, PERT diagrams are a better choice.

CASE STUDY: Remodeling Project

Project: Remodel Building 7 to add four new offices by the end of the third quarter at a cost not to exceed $40,000.

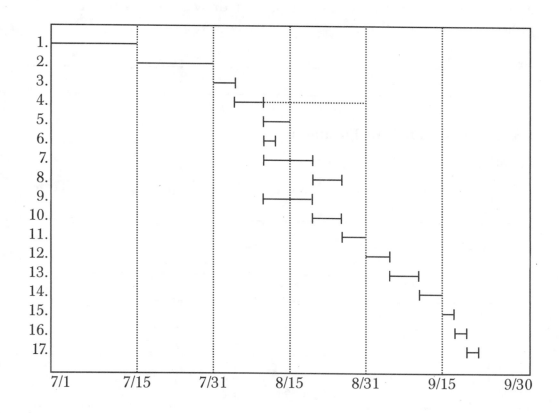

Project Steps, with Time Estimates

1. Complete working plans	15	10. Install heating/AC	5
2. Obtain building permit	16	11. Install insulation	5
3. Pour foundation	5	12. Install sheetrock	5
4. Frame walls/roof	5	13. Install doors/trim	5
5. Install roofing	5	14. Paint interior	3
6. Frame/install windows	1	15. Install electrical fixtures	2
7. Install exterior siding	10	16. Cleanup	3
8. Paint exterior	3	17. Install floor covering	2
9. Install electrical wiring	10		

PRACTICE DRAWING A GANTT CHART

Using the project for which you prepared a work breakdown structure, estimate the time required for each step. Then draw a Gantt chart for the project.

Project: _____

_____

Project Steps, with Time Estimates

(Total time: _____)

Step	Time	Step	Time
_____	____	_____	____
_____	____	_____	____
_____	____	_____	____
_____	____	_____	____
_____	____	_____	____
_____	____	_____	____

Gantt Chart

PERT Diagrams

PERT stands for Program Evaluation and Review Technique. It is a more sophisticated form of planning than a Gantt chart, and is appropriate for projects with many interactive steps. A PERT diagram has three components:

➤ Events are represented by circles.

➤ Activities are represented by arrows connecting the events.

➤ Non-activities connecting two events are shown as dotted-line arrows. (A non-activity represents a dependency between two events for which no work is required.)

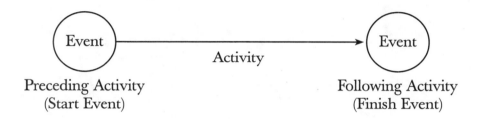

PERT diagrams are most useful if the amount of time scheduled for completing an activity is included on the activity line. Time is recorded in a unit appropriate to the project; days are most common, but hours, weeks, or even months are occasionally used. Some diagrams show two numbers for time estimates—a high estimate and a low estimate.

The most sophisticated PERT diagrams are drawn on a time scale, with the horizontal projection of connecting arrows drawn to represent the amount of time required for each activity. In the process of diagramming to scale, some connecting arrows will be longer than completion of that task requires. This represents slack time in the project and is depicted by a heavy dot at the end of the appropriate time period, followed by a dotted-line arrow pointing to the following event.

PERT Diagram Drawn to Time Scale

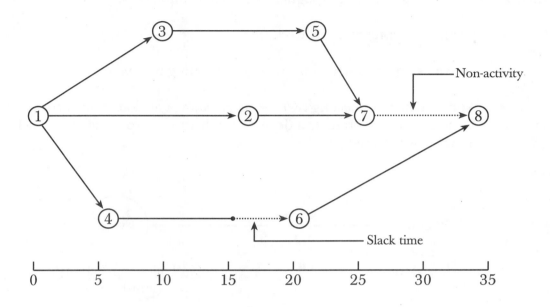

To draw a PERT diagram, list the steps required to finish a project and estimate the time required to complete each step. Then draw a network of relationships among the steps, keeping in mind the importance of proper sequencing. Numbers corresponding to the steps on your list are written in appropriate event circles to identify each step. The time to complete the next step is shown on the arrow. Steps that can be under way at the same time are shown on different paths. Be sure to include all the elements from your work breakdown structure.

A PERT diagram not only shows the relationship among various steps in a project, but also serves as an easy way to calculate the critical path. The critical path is the longest path through the network and as such identifies essential steps that must be completed on time to avoid delays in completing the project. The critical path is shown as a heavy line in the following example.

The usefulness of a PERT diagram can be increased by coloring each step as it is completed. Actual time can be written over the estimated time to maintain a running tally of actual versus planned time along the critical path.

CASE STUDY: Remodeling Project

Project: Remodel Building 7 to add four new offices by the end of the third quarter at a cost not to exceed $40,000.

Note: Numbers in the circles correspond to the steps listed below. Numbers on the lines show the days required to complete the step that follows.

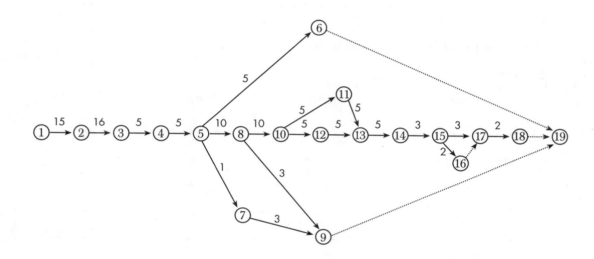

Project Steps, with Time Estimates (in days)

1. Project started	–	11. Heating/air conditioning in	5
2. Working plans completed	15	12. Insulation installed	5
3. Building permit obtained	16	13. Sheetrock hung	5
4. Foundation poured	5	14. Interior doors/trim installed	5
5. Walls/roof framed	5	15. Interior painted	3
6. Roofing completed	5	16. Electrical fixtures installed	2
7. Windows installed	1	17. Cleanup completed	3
8. Exterior siding installed	10	18. Floor covering installed	2
9. Exterior painted	3	19. Project completed	–
10. Electrical wiring in	10		

PRACTICE DRAWING A PERT DIAGRAM

You have already selected a project, broken it down into steps, and estimated the time required to complete each step. Now you're ready to draw a PERT diagram for the project.

Project: _____

_____

Project Steps with Time Estimates

(Total time: _____)

Step	Time	Step	Time
_____	_____	_____	_____
_____	_____	_____	_____
_____	_____	_____	_____
_____	_____	_____	_____
_____	_____	_____	_____
_____	_____	_____	_____

PERT Diagram

Planning the Cost Dimension

There are many reasons to plan carefully for project costs. To begin with, if you overestimate costs you may lose the job before you begin because your rates are not competitive. A good plan includes identifying sources of supplies and materials, and this research will help assure that estimated costs are realistic. The main function of a good budget is to monitor the costs of a project while it is in progress and to avoid cost overruns.

Some inaccuracies in a budget are inevitable, but they should not be the consequence of insufficient attention while drafting the original plan. The goal is to be as realistic as possible.

You cannot estimate the cost of your project until you know how long it will take, since labor is typically the most significant cost item. Therefore, use your work breakdown structure and project schedule as the starting point for developing your project budget.

Typical costs components:

> **Labor**   > **Equipment rental**

> **Overhead**   > **General and administrative**

> **Materials**   > **Profit (if applicable)**

> **Supplies**

Cost Components Defined

➤ **Labor:** The wages paid to all staff working directly on the project for the time spent on it.

➤ **Overhead:** The cost of payroll taxes and fringe benefits for everyone working directly on the project for the time spent on it. Usually calculated as a percentage of direct labor cost.

➤ **Materials:** The cost of items purchased for use in the project. Includes such things as lumber, cement, steel, nails, screws, rivets, bolts, and paint.

➤ **Supplies:** The cost of tools, equipment, office supplies, and so on needed for the project. If something has a useful life beyond the project, its cost should be prorated.

➤ **Equipment rental:** The cost of renting equipment such as scaffolding, compressors, cranes, bulldozers, and trucks for use on the project.

➤ **General and administrative:** The cost of management and support services such as purchasing, accounting, and secretarial for time dedicated to the project. Usually calculated as a percentage of project cost.

➤ **Profit:** In a for-profit project, the reward to the firm for successfully completing the project. Usually calculated as a percentage of project cost.

With the cost components identified and the project broken down into steps, create a worksheet to tally the costs for the total project.

Note that the cost of a step or subunit is sometimes simplified if it is to be sub-contracted. The cost includes bidding the work, selecting a contractor, and then using the contract price as your cost.

CASE STUDY: Remodeling Project

Project Cost Worksheet
(Prepared by general contractor)

Step	Labor	Over-head	Materials	Supplies	Equipment Rental	Gen & Admin	Profit	Total
1. Complete working plans	800	320		200		52.80	274.56	1,647.36
2. Obtain building permit	200	80				11.20	58.24	349.44
3. Pour foundation	2,600	1,040	1,800	200	200	233.60	1,214.72	7,288.32
4. Frame walls/roof	700	420	900			80.80	420.16	2,520.96
5. Install roofing	900	360	1,400			106.40	553.28	3,319.68
6. Frame/install windows	800	320	1,200	50	300	106.80	555.36	3,332.16
7. Install exterior siding	800	320	1,400			100.80	524.16	3,144.96
8. Paint exterior	400	160	220	50	250	43.20	224.64	1,347.84
9. Install electrical wiring	600	240	700			61.60	320.32	1,921.92
10. Install heating/AC	1,400	560	1,800			150.40	782.08	4,692.48
11. Install insulation	300	120	600			40.80	212.16	1,272.96
12. Install sheetrock	800	320	400			60.80	316.16	1,896.96
13. Install doors/trim	320	128	1,400			73.92	384.38	2,306.30
14. Paint interior	400	160	250			32.40	168.48	1,010.88
15. Install electrical fixtures	200	80	650			37.20	193.44	1,160.64
16. Cleanup	300	120	50			18.80	97.76	586.56
17. Install floor covering	240	96	1,400	500	750	69.44	361.09	2,166.53
Total	11,760	4,844	14,170			1,280.96	6,660.99	39,965.95

Potential Budget Problems

➤ The impact of inflation on long-term projects

➤ The impact of currency exchange rates on international projects

➤ Failure to obtain firm price commitments from suppliers and subcontractors

➤ Poorly prepared work breakdowns structures that lead to incomplete budgets

➤ "Fudge factors" built into internal support group estimates

➤ Estimates based on different methods of cost analysis, i.e., hours versus dollars

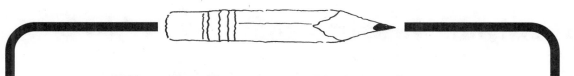

PRACTICE ESTIMATING PROJECT COSTS

Prepare a cost estimate for the project you have been using. Use as many of the cost columns as apply.

Subunit or step								
Total								

Assigning Responsibility

Determining who has responsibility for completing each step of a project should be done as early as possible so that the leaders can participate in planning schedules and budgets. Participation leads to a greater commitment to achieve the project within time and cost limitations.

The number of people involved in a project varies with its size and scope. Sometimes one person is responsible for more than one step.

To make the best use of your resources when deciding who is responsible for a portion of your project, broaden your point of view to include subcontractors and service departments, as well as project team members.

PRACTICE MAKING A PLANNING SUMMARY WORKSHEET

Select a project, break it down into its steps or subunits, estimate the time required and cost for each unit, and identify the person or group responsible for carrying it out.

Project: _____

_____

Component or Step	Budget	Schedule	Responsibility

Progress Review: Part 3

Write **T** for True or **F** for False in response to each of the following statements.

1. __ Planning is not necessary on small projects.

2. __ A work breakdown structure is the starting point for planning a project.

3. __ Job specifications detail the requirements for project quality.

4. __ Tests should be a part of specifications.

5. __ When developing a project schedule, the duration and sequence of each step is important.

6. __ The latest time a step can begin is not significant in the planning process.

7. __ Experience is the only basis for estimating time requirements.

8. __ A Gantt chart graphically displays the time relationship of each step in a project.

9. __ A Gantt chart clearly displays the interdependencies of project steps.

10. __ A PERT diagram is more sophisticated than a Gantt chart.

11. __ The critical path is the shortest total time through a PERT diagram.

12. __ In cost planning, overhead includes general and administrative expenses.

13. __ Those responsible for steps of a project should not be included in planning.

14. __ Training project personnel is the responsibility of the human resources department, and therefore should not be a concern for the project manager.

15. __ Establishing project policies and responsibilities is a part of project planning.

Implementing
the Plan

What Happens in the Implementation Stage?

During the implementation phase, the project manager coordinates all the project elements. This involves a number of responsibilities, including controlling work in progress to see that it is carried out according to plan; providing feedback to the team working on the project; negotiating for materials, supplies, and services; and resolving differences among those involved with the project. These responsibilities require a variety of skills. This section presents tools and techniques to help project managers during the implementation stage.

Key duties during implementation:

> **Controlling work in progress**

> **Providing feedback**

> **Negotiating for materials, supplies, and services**

> **Resolving differences**

Controlling Work in Progress

Controlling is the central activity during implementation. The most important tool in this process is the plan that was developed to define the project parameters for specifications, schedule, and budget. These are the standards against which performance is measured. Controlling involves three steps, each of which is discussed in detail in the pages that follow:

1. **Establishing standards**

2. **Monitoring performance**

3. **Taking corrective action**

STEP 1
Establishing Standards

Standards for the project were set in the project specifications created as part of the planning stage. The project manager must constantly refer to these specifications and make sure the project team is also referencing them. If the project deviates from the original specifications, there is no guarantee that the success predicted by the feasibility studies will actually happen and the product or project outcome might fail to meet performance standards.

A number of tools are available to help project managers control the project and make sure that the parameters defined in the specifications for quality, time, and budget are actually being met. A Gantt chart or PERT diagram developed at the planning stage is a great device for tracking how the time dimension of the project is proceeding in relationship to the plan.

In the following pages you'll learn about four additional charts that are useful for project control:

➤ **Control Point Identification Charts**

➤ **Project Control Charts**

➤ **Milestone Charts**

➤ **Budget Control Charts**

Control Point Identification Charts

A helpful technique for controlling a project is to invest some time thinking through what is likely to go wrong in each of the three project parameters. Then identify when and how you will know that something is amiss and what you will do to correct the problem if it occurs. This will help minimize the likelihood that you will be caught by surprise, as well as save time in responding to the problem. A control point identification chart is an easy way to summarize this information.

Example of a Control Point Identification Chart

Control Element	What is likely to go wrong?	How and when will I know?	What will I do about it?
Quality	Workmanship might be less than desired.	Upon personal inspection of each stage of project.	Have substandard work redone.
Cost	Cost of any subunit may exceed budget.	When purchase agreements are made.	First, seek alternative suppliers, then consider alternative materials.
Timeliness	Time to complete any step may exceed schedule.	By closely monitoring actual progress against schedule along critical path.	Look for ways to improve efficiency, attempt to capture time from later steps, authorize overtime if budget permits.

PRACTICE MAKING A CONTROL POINT IDENTIFICATION CHART

Select a project and think through each of the questions relating to the three project parameters.

Project: _____

_____

Control Element	What is likely to go wrong?	How and when will I know?	What will I do about it?
Quality			
Cost			
Timeliness			

Project Control Charts

Another helpful tool is a project control chart, which uses budget and schedule plans to give a quick status report of the project. It compares actual to planned, calculates a variance on each subunit completed, and tallies a cumulative variance for the project.

To prepare a project control chart, refer to the work breakdown and list all subunits or steps for the project. Then, use the schedule to list the time planned to complete each step, and use the budget to list the expected cost of each step.

As each step is completed, record its actual time and actual cost. Calculate variances and carry the cumulative total forward.

This technique can be put into a spreadsheet on your personal computer. Large projects within a company may be able to use the company's computerized accounting system to create a report that uses cost and schedule data routinely captured for other purposes.

CASE STUDY: Remodeling Project

Project Control Chart

Project: Remodel Building 7 to add four new offices by the end of the third quarter at a cost not to exceed $40,000.

Project Steps	Cost				Schedule			
	Budget	Actual	Variance	Total	Planned	Actual	Variance	Total
1. Complete working plans	1,600	1,650	50	50	15	15	–	–
2. Obtain building permit	350	350	–	50	16	15	(1)	(1)
3. Pour foundation	7,000	7,200	200	250	5	3	(2)	(3)
4. Frame walls/roof	650	700	50	300	5	5	–	(3)
5. Install roofing	3,400	3,300	(100)	200	5*	6	1	(3)
6. Frame/install windows	3,400	3,300	(100)	100	1*	1	–	(3)
7. Install exterior siding	3,200	3,150	(50)	50	10	9	(1)	(4)
8. Paint exterior	1,400	1,300	(100)	(150)	3			
9. Install electrical wiring	2,000				10*			
10. Install heating/AC	4,700				5			
11. Install insulation	1,300				5			
12. Install sheetrock	1,900				5			
13. Install doors/trim	2,400				5			
14. Paint interior	1,000				3			
15. Install electrical fixtures	1,200				2			
16. Cleanup	600				3			
17. Install floor covering	2,200				2			
18. Project completion (Total)	38,300				84			

*Not on critical path—excluded from total.

Note: If you prefer over-budget and schedule amounts to be negative numbers, subtract actual from budget and planned. Under-budget and schedule amounts will then be positive numbers.

PROJECT CONTROL CHART

Project Steps	Cost				Schedule			
	Budget	Actual	Variance	Total	Planned	Actual	Variance	Total

Milestone Charts

A milestone chart presents a broad-brush picture of a project's schedule and control dates. It lists those key events that are clearly verifiable by others or that require approval before the project can proceed. If this is done correctly, a project will not have many milestones. Because of this lack of detail, a milestone chart is not very helpful during the planning phase when more information is required. However, it is particularly useful in the implementation phase because it provides a concise summary of progress that has been made.

Example of a Milestone Chart

Milestone	Scheduled Completion	Actual Completion
1. Foundation completed	August 5	August 2
2. Framing completed	August 10	August 7
3. Exterior finished	August 25	
4. Electrical wiring completed	August 20	
5. Heating and A/C installed	August 25	
6. Interior finished	September 22	

Budget Control Charts

Budget control charts are generally of two varieties. One lists the project steps or subunits with actual costs compared to budget. It is similar to project control charts, which were discussed earlier, and can be generated by hand or computer. The other kind is a graph of budgeted costs compared to actual. Either bar or line graphs may be used. Bar graphs usually relate budgeted and actual costs by project steps, while line graphs usually relate planned cumulative project costs to actual costs over time.

Example of a Budget Control Chart

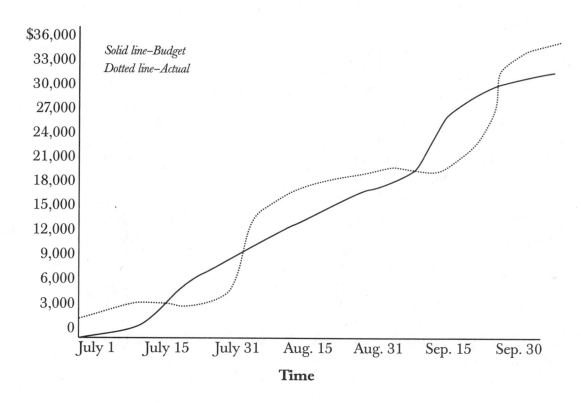

Another helpful approach to budget control is to compare the percentage of budget spent to the percentage of project completed. The data can be compared by making a list or a graph. While the percentage of budget spent is a precise figure, the percentage of project completed should be estimated by someone familiar with the project and its progress.

STEP 2
Monitoring Performance

The heart of the control process is monitoring work in progress. It is your way to know what is going on-how actual compares to plan. With effective monitoring, you will know if and when corrective action is required. Following are ways to keep abreast of project progress:

Inspection is probably the most common way to monitor project performance. It is handled by trained inspectors as well as by the project manager. Get out into the area where the work is performed and observe what is going on. Inspection is an effective way to see whether project specifications are being met, as well as whether there is unnecessary waste or unsafe work practices. Inspections should be unannounced and on a random schedule. However, they should also be open and direct. Ask questions and listen to explanations.

Interim progress reviews are communications between the project manager and those responsible for the various steps of a project. Progress reviews can be in a group or on an individual basis, and either face-to-face or by telephone. Alternatively, progress reports can be submitted in writing. Progress reviews typically occur on a fixed time schedule—daily or weekly—or are keyed to the completion of individual project steps. These scheduled reviews are typically augmented by reviews called by either the project manager or the one responsible for the work. (Guidelines for conducting progress reviews follow.)

Testing is another way to verify project quality. Certain tests are usually written into the specifications to confirm that the desired quality is being achieved. Typical tests include pressure or stress tests on mechanical components.

Auditing can be done during the course of a project or at its conclusion. Common areas for audit are financial record-keeping, purchasing practices, safety practices, security practices, maintenance procedures, and authority for disbursement. Auditors should be experts in the area of the project under review, and typically are not members of the project team. After carefully examining the area under review, a report is written describing in detail what was found and pointing out practices that deviate from established policy, authorized procedures, or sound business practices.

Effective monitoring includes more than one source of information. In addition to data from records, a combination of inspections, progress reviews, testing, and auditing will round out your information and keep you up-to-date on the status of your project.

Conducting Interim Progress Reviews

Interim progress reviews typically occur on a fixed time schedule, such as daily or weekly. They also may occur when some problem is observed or at the completion of a significant step. Three topics are usually on the agenda:

➤ Review of progress against plan

➤ Review of problems encountered and how they were handled

➤ Review of anticipated problems with proposed plans for handling them

The project manager's role during an interim progress review is to achieve the objectives of knowing the status of operations and influencing the course of future events as necessary. During the discussion, the project manager may take on any of the following roles:

Listener

Listen as an individual updates you on progress, deviation from plan, problems encountered, and solutions proposed. Listen not only to what is said, but also how it's said. Is the person excited, frustrated, discouraged? Help clarify what is being said by asking questions, and verify what you think is being said by restating your understanding of both facts and feelings.

Contributor

In many interim reviews, progress is in line with plans. However, you occasionally will have problems to deal with. When this occurs, you can contribute to their solution by directing the other person toward possible courses of action. Use your knowledge and experience as necessary to move the project forward.

Integrator

An important role of a project manager is to integrate the individual parts of a project into a compatible whole. Is something being neglected? Is there a duplication of effort? How can available resources be best deployed?

Leader

Perhaps the most important role for the project manager is that of leader. Through a variety of techniques, you must keep the team's effort directed toward the common goal of completing the project according to specifications, on time, and within budget. You must confirm and recognize good performance, correct poor performance, and keep interest and enthusiasm high.

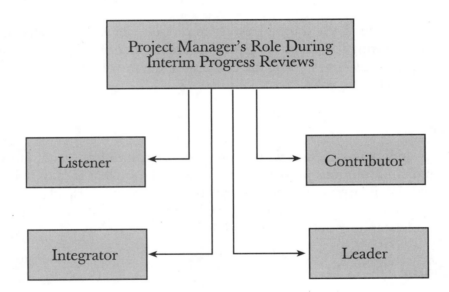

STEP 3
Taking Corrective Action

As a project progresses and you monitor performance, there will be times when actual does not measure up to plan. This calls for corrective action. However, don't be too quick to take action. Some deficiencies are self-correcting. It is unrealistic to expect steady and consistent progress day after day. Sometimes you'll fall behind and sometimes you'll be ahead, but in a well-planned project, you will probably finish on schedule and within budget.

When quality is not according to specification, the customary action is to do it over according to plan. However, this needs to be more closely examined in some instances. For example, if the work or material exceeds specifications, you may choose to accept it. If it falls short, you need to consider how much it deviates from specifications and whether the deficiency will cause the project to fail its performance evaluation. The final decision may be to have the work redone, but that is not an automatic outcome.

When the project begins to fall behind schedule, there are three alternatives that may correct the problem. The first is to examine the work remaining to be done and decide whether the lost time can be recovered in the next steps. If this is not feasible, consider offering an incentive for on-time completion of the project. The incentive could be justified if you compare this expenditure to potential losses due to late completion. Finally, consider deploying more resources. This too will cost more, but may offset further losses from delayed completion.

When the project begins to exceed budget, consider the work remaining and whether or not cost overruns can be recouped on work yet to be completed. If this isn't practical, consider narrowing the project scope or obtaining more funding from your client.

What to Do When You Start Falling Behind

The Xs in the **Cost** and **Schedule** columns indicate actions that could be effective in dealing with these parameters.

Action	Cost	Schedule
1. **Renegotiate.** Discuss with your client the prospect of increasing the budget for the project or extending the deadline for completion.	X	X
2. **Recover during later steps.** If you begin to fall behind in the early steps of a project, reexamine budgets and schedules for later steps. Perhaps you can save on later steps so the overall budget and/or schedule will be met.	X	X
3. **Narrow project scope.** Perhaps nonessential elements of the project can be eliminated, thereby reducing costs and/or saving time.	X	X
4. **Deploy more resources.** You may need to put more people or machines on the project to meet a critical schedule. Increased costs must be weighed against the importance of the deadline.		X
5. **Accept substitution.** When something is not available or is more expensive than budgeted, substituting a comparable item may solve your problem.	X	X
6. **Seek alternative sources.** When a supplier can't deliver within budget or schedule, look for others who can. (You may choose to accept a substitute rather than seek other sources.)	X	X
7. **Accept partial delivery.** Sometimes a supplier can deliver a partial order to keep your project on schedule and complete the delivery later.		X
8. **Offer incentives.** Go beyond the scope of the original contract and offer a bonus or other incentive for on-time delivery.		X
9. **Demand compliance.** Sometimes demanding that people do what they agreed to do gets the desired results. You may have to appeal to higher management for backing and support.	X	X

Providing Feedback

Project managers can find many opportunities to provide feedback to those who have a hand in completing the project. Through feedback, individuals learn about the effect their behavior has on others and on the project's success. It serves to maintain good performance and correct poor performance. To be effective, however, feedback must be handled properly. This illustration shows the continuous loop that exists when there is good feedback.

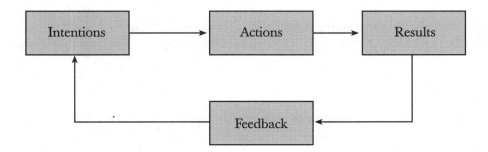

The most important guideline when providing feedback is to deal only with what you can observe. This limits your conversation to actions and results, because you cannot observe someone's intentions.

When offering positive feedback, describe the actions and results in a straightforward way and include an appropriate statement of your reaction. For example, you might tell someone, "By staying late last night and finishing the work you were doing, the project was able to move forward on schedule. I appreciate your putting out the extra effort."

Negative feedback can be handled in the same manner, but an important element is missing, which is how the team member should deal with similar situations in the future. The following sequence should prove more effective.

Handling negative feedback:

➤ Describe the observed actions and results. Ask the individual if those were his or her intended results.

➤ With a typical "No" response, ask what different actions would likely produce the desired results.

➤ Discuss alternative courses of action.

➤ Agree upon a way to handle similar situations if they should occur in the future.

Check Your Feedback Style

Rate yourself by placing a check in front of each action that is typical of how you handle giving feedback. The ones you don't check represent opportunities for development.

❏ **Describe rather than evaluate.** By describing observed action and results, the individual is free to use or not use the information. By avoiding evaluation, you reduce the likelihood of a defensive reaction.

❏ **Be specific rather than general.** Avoid using "always" and "never." Rather, discuss specific times and events. Avoid generalized conclusions such as, "you're too dominating." Rather, be specific by saying, "When you don't listen to others, you may miss a valuable idea."

❏ **Deal with behavior that can be changed.** Frustration is increased when you remind someone of a shortcoming over which he or she has no control.

❏ **Be timely.** Generally, feedback is most useful at the earliest opportunity after the behavior.

❏ **Communicate clearly.** This is particularly important when handling negative feedback. One way to ensure clear communication is to have the receiver rephrase the feedback to see if it corresponds to what you had in mind.

Negotiating for Materials, Supplies, and Services

Negotiating is an important process that takes up as much as 20% of a manager's time. Negotiating is a way to resolve differences, and it can contribute significantly to the success of your project.

The ideas presented here will prepare you to negotiate effectively.

Negotiation

Negotiation is a discussion between two parties with a goal of reaching agreement on issues that separate them when neither party has the power (or the desire to use its power) to force an outcome.

For an excellent book on this topic, read Successful Negotiation *by Robert B. Maddux, Crisp Publications.*

Ten Guidelines for Effective Negotiation

1 Prepare.

Do your homework. Know what outcome you want and why. Find out what outcome the other party wants. Avoid negotiating when you are not prepared—ask for the time you need. As part of your preparation, figure out what you will do if you are unable to come to an agreement. Your power in negotiation develops from attractive alternatives—the greater your ability to walk away, the stronger your bargaining position.

2 Minimize perceptual differences.

The way you see something can be quite different from how the other party sees it. Don't assume you know the other person's view. Ask questions to gain understanding and restate your understanding so it can be confirmed or corrected by the other party.

3 Listen.

Active, attentive listening is mandatory to effective negotiation. Let the other side have an equal share of the airtime. (If you're talking more than 50% of the time, you are not listening enough.) In the process, respect silence. Occasionally people need to collect their thoughts before moving ahead. Don't try to fill this time with talking.

4 Take notes.

You need to know where you are—what has been agreed to and what remains to be resolved. Don't rely on memory. Take notes and then summarize your agreement in a memorandum.

5 Be creative.

Early closure and criticism stifle creative thinking. Be willing to set some time aside to explore different and unusual ways to solve your problem. During this time, do not permit criticism of ideas offered. All negotiations can benefit from nonjudgmental creative thinking.

6 Help the other party.

Good negotiators recognize that the other party's problem is their problem as well. Put yourself in the other's position and work to find a solution that meets everyone's needs. After all, no agreement will hold up unless both parties support it.

7 Make good trade-offs.

Avoid giving something for nothing. At least get some goodwill or an obligation for future payback. The basic principle to follow is to trade what is cheap to you but valuable to the other party for what is valuable to you but cheap to the other party.

8 Be quick to apologize.

An apology is the quickest, surest way to de-escalate negative feelings. It need not be a personal apology. An apology for the situation you're in can be just as effective. Also, don't contribute to hostility by making hostile remarks. Hostility takes the discussion away from the issues and shifts it to a defense of self where the goal is to destroy the opponent.

9 Avoid ultimatums.

An ultimatum requires the other party to either surrender or fight. Neither outcome will contribute to future cooperation. Avoid boxing someone in. This happens when you offer only two alternatives, neither of which is desirable to the other person.

10 Set realistic deadlines.

Many negotiations continue too long because no deadline exists. A deadline requires both sides to be economical in their use of time. It permits you to question the value of certain discussion topics and encourages both sides to consider concessions and trade-offs in order to meet deadlines.

Resolving Differences

What is best for one department or group won't necessarily be best for others. Out of these differences can come creative solutions when the situation is handled properly. Skill in resolving differences is an important quality for successful project managers.

Consider the model on the following page. Differences can be resolved my way, your way, or our way. As a result, four strategies emerge.

Strategies for resolving differences:

➤ **Demanding**

➤ **Problem solving**

➤ **Bargaining**

➤ **Giving in**

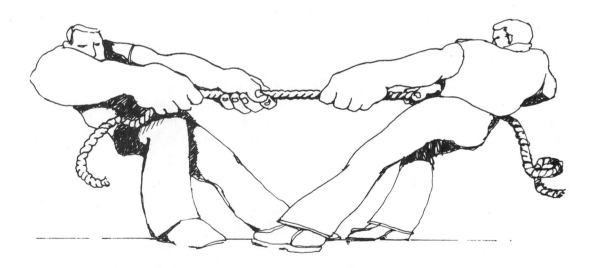

Model for Resolving Differences

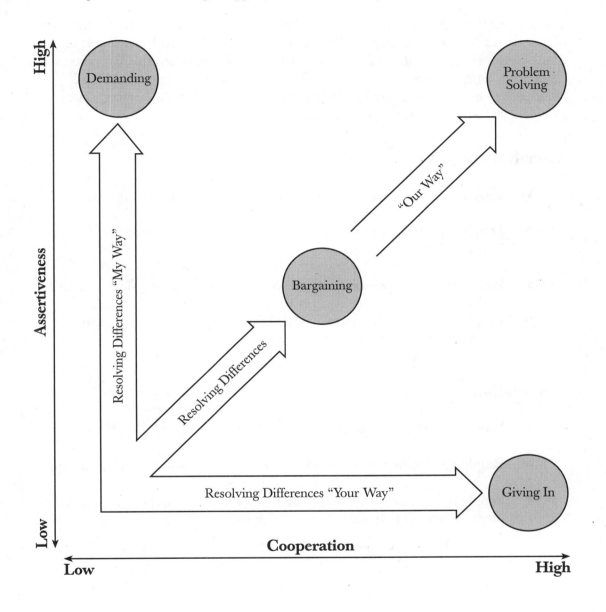

The strategy one chooses to resolve differences tends to result from an interplay of assertiveness and cooperation. This process can be clouded by emotion at times, and it is difficult to achieve a satisfactory outcome when this happens. Therefore, when you sense that either the other person's or your thinking is clouded by emotion, ask to delay discussion for a while. The following issues influence assertiveness and cooperation.

Assertiveness

➤ People tend to be more assertive when an issue is important to them.

➤ People tend to be more assertive when they are confident of their knowledge.

➤ People tend to be more assertive when things are going against them.

➤ People tend to be less assertive when they feel they are at a power disadvantage.

Cooperation

➤ People tend to be more cooperative when they respect the other person.

➤ People tend to be more cooperative when they value the relationship.

➤ People tend to be more cooperative when they are dependent on the other person to help carry out the decision.

Strategies for Resolving Differences

Given the interplay of assertiveness and cooperation, the following strategies are common for resolving differences.

Demanding

Demanding is high in assertiveness and low in cooperation. It suggests confidence and that the issue is important, coupled with a lack of concern for the relationship and no dependency on the other person.

Problem Solving

Problem solving is high in assertiveness, coupled with high cooperation. It suggests that the issue is important and that there is the need for an ongoing relationship with the other person.

Bargaining

Bargaining is moderate in both assertiveness and cooperation. It suggests that an important issue is being addressed by equally powerful parties. Each must be willing to give a little to reach agreement. Bargaining is also an appropriate backup strategy when joint problem solving seems unattainable.

Giving In

Giving in is low in assertiveness and high in cooperation. The issue may be unimportant to you, you may lack knowledge, or you may simply want to go along with the other person's proposal in order to build up the relationship between you.

Each strategy has its place. However, too few people recognize the conditions that support each strategy. Many people adopt one approach for resolving differences and use it in all situations. Obviously, it will be ineffective in many cases. Learn to distinguish among the various types of situations and adopt an approach that has the greatest chance of success in the long run. Don't overlook the importance of maintaining cooperative relationships.

Common Sources of Differences in Project Management

➤ **Allocation of human resources.** With limited personnel, project managers often have different views than others have on how staff will be assigned.

➤ **Use of equipment and facilities.** Project managers often differ with others over the use of equipment and facilities that must be shared.

➤ **Costs.** As you work at controlling costs against the approved project budget, you will often encounter conflict with suppliers who feel a need to increase costs over their original commitment.

➤ **Technical opinions.** Frequently there will be different opinions on how something ought to be done.

➤ **Administrative procedures.** Administrative procedures often become points of difference, especially when not followed.

➤ **Responsibilities.** There will be occasions when more than one person claims an area of responsibility and other occasions when no one wants to accept responsibility.

➤ **Scheduling.** Differences will develop around schedules and deadlines. Others you depend on will not deliver on their commitments.

➤ **Priorities.** There will be differences about which things are more important and, therefore, which should be handled first.

Progress Review: Part 4

Write **T** for True or **F** for False in response to each of the following statements.

1. __ Negotiating for materials, supplies, and services is not a part of a project manager's duties.

2. __ Controlling is the central activity during the implementation phase of a project.

3. __ Specifications, schedules, and budgets developed during the planning phase become the standards against which actual progress is measured in the implementation phase.

4. __ Control point identification usually does not save time.

5. __ A project control chart summarizes information on the quality dimension of a project.

6. __ A milestone chart is less detailed than required for project planning.

7. __ Budget data does not adapt to a line graph presentation for monitoring progress.

8. __ Testing provides important information on the quality dimension of a project.

9. __ Personal inspection is the least effective way to monitor project progress.

10. __ Audits are done only at the end of projects to see whether the project is over budget.

11. __ An interim progress review requires good listening skills.

12. __ All off-specification work should be redone.

13. __ Lost time can often be made up on later steps of the project.

14. __ Deploying more resources may save money for the client in the long run.

15. __ It is never acceptable to renegotiate the terms of the project after it is under way.

16. __ Effective feedback focuses on actions, results, and reaction to them.

17. __ It is not important to communicate clearly when giving feedback, because the other person already knows what you are talking about.

18. __ Successful negotiating requires a power advantage over the other person.

19. __ You have power in negotiation when you have attractive alternatives.

20. __ Giving in is never an acceptable strategy for resolving differences.

Score Your Responses

1.	F	5.	F	9.	F	13.	T	17.	F
2.	T	6.	T	10.	F	14.	T	18.	F
3.	T	7.	F	11.	T	15.	F	19.	T
4.	F	8.	T	12.	F	16.	T	20.	F

12 to 15 Excellent: You're ready to move on.
9 to 11 Good: A quick review would be helpful before you proceed.
0 to 8 Poor: You must have dozed off. Reread Parts 1 and 2.

Completing the Project

Bringing the Project to a Successful Conclusion

The goal of project management is to obtain client acceptance of the project's end result. This means that the client agrees that the quality specifications of the project parameters were met. In order to have the acceptance stage go smoothly, the client and project manager must have well-documented criteria for judging performance in place from the beginning of the project. This is not to say that the criteria has not changed since project inception, but when changes were made, the contract should have been amended to list specification changes, along with any resulting changes in schedule and budget.

Objective, measurable criteria are always best, while subjective criteria are risky and subject to interpretation. There should be no room for doubt or ambiguity, although this is often difficult to achieve. It is also important to be clear about what the project output is expected to accomplish. For instance, the following three outcomes may produce entirely different results: the product performs the specified functions; it was built according to approved design; or it solves the client's problem.

The project may or may not be complete when results are delivered to the client. Often there are documentation requirements, such as operation manuals, completed drawings, and a final report, that still have to be provided. Staff may need to be trained to operate the new facility or product, and a final audit is common.

Finally, project team members need to be reassigned; surplus equipment, materials, and supplies disposed of; and facilities released.

The final step of any project should be an evaluation review. This is a look back over the project to see what was learned that will contribute to the success of future projects. This review is best done by the core project team and typically in a group discussion.

Project Completion Checklist

- ❑ Test project output to see that it works.
- ❑ Write operations manual.
- ❑ Complete final drawings.
- ❑ Deliver project output to client.
- ❑ Train client's personnel to operate project output.
- ❑ Reassign project personnel.
- ❑ Dispose of surplus equipment, materials, and supplies.
- ❑ Release facilities.
- ❑ Summarize major problems encountered and their solutions.
- ❑ Document technological advances made.
- ❑ Summarize recommendations for future research and development.
- ❑ Summarize lessons learned in dealing with interfaces.
- ❑ Write performance evaluation reports on all project staff.
- ❑ Provide feedback on performance to all project staff.
- ❑ Complete final audit.
- ❑ Write final report.
- ❑ Conduct project review with upper management.
- ❑ Declare the project complete.

Project Evaluation Form

1. How close to scheduled completion was the project actually completed?

2. What did we learn about scheduling that will help us on our next project?

3. How close to budget was the final cost?

4. What did we learn about budgeting that will help us on our next project?

5. Upon completion, did the project output meet client specifications without additional work?

6. If additional work was required, please describe:

_____

_____

_____

7. What did we learn about writing specifications that will help us on our next project?

_____

_____

_____

8. What did we learn about staffing that will help us on our next project?

_____

_____

_____

9. What did we learn about monitoring performance that will help us on our next project?

_____

_____

_____

10. What did we learn about taking corrective action that will help us on our next project?

_____

_____

_____

11. What technological advances were made on this project?

_____

_____

_____

12. What tools and techniques were developed that will be useful on our next project?

_____

_____

_____

13. What recommendations do we have for future research and development?

_____

_____

_____

14. What lessons did we learn from our dealings with service organizations and outside vendors?

_____

_____

_____

15. If we had the opportunity to do the project over, what would we do differently?

_____

_____

_____

Progress Review: Part 5

Write **T** for True or **F** for False in response to each of the following statements.

1. __ The work of a project manager ends with the delivery of the project output to the client.

2. __ The criteria for evaluating performance must be agreed to by the client before the project gets under way.

3. __ Objective, measurable criteria of performance are easy to develop.

4. __ Writing operations manuals and training client personnel in the operation of project output are part of the completion phase.

5. __ There is usually no surplus equipment, materials, or supplies to worry about at the end of a project.

6. __ The reassignment of project team personnel is one of the final steps in closing down a project.

7. __ Typically, the completion of a final audit and the writing of a final report conclude the project manager's responsibilities.

8. __ After a project is completed, little can be gained from spending time evaluating the experience.

9. __ Projects often make technological advances that are worth sharing with other parts of the organization.

10. __ If they are not recorded, lessons learned during the course of a project are typically lost and must be relearned by future project managers.

Summary

A Model for Successful Project Management

Projects are temporary undertakings that have a definite beginning and end. This feature distinguishes them from the ongoing work of an organization. There are four phases in any successful project: defining, planning, implementing, and completing. The diagram shown on page 88 summarizes these phases.

It is imperative to the success of a project that it be clearly defined before it is undertaken. Any definition should include the criteria for determining successful completion of the project. It is reasonable to expect changes to occur once the project is under way, but these changes should be documented along with any resulting impact on schedule and budget.

A successful project produces an outcome that performs as expected, by deadline, and within cost limits. Thus, the three parameters by which a project is planned and controlled are established. Quality is defined by specifications, time is defined by schedule, and costs are defined by budget.

To carry out the work of the project, a temporary team is usually assembled. This necessitates developing an organization, assigning duties and responsibilities, and training people in their duties. Frequently, policies and procedures are required to clarify how the team is to function during the project.

When work on the project begins, the project manager has many responsibilities. The efforts of different individuals and groups must be coordinated so that things run smoothly, and the progress of the project must be monitored and measured against plans. When deviations occur, corrective action must be taken. Also, project managers are expected to provide feedback to team members, negotiate for materials, supplies, and service, and help resolve differences that occur.

The goal of the project is to deliver an outcome to the client. When that day finally arrives, there are still things to be done before the project is complete. This can include writing operations manuals, training client personnel to use the project output, reassigning project personnel, disposing of surplus equipment, materials, and supplies, evaluating the experience, completing a final audit, writing a project report, and conducting a project review with upper management.

Not every project requires the same attention to each of these activities. It will depend upon the type of project you are undertaking, its size and scope, and the type of organization you are affiliated with. Use your own judgment in selecting the steps important to the success of your project.

Best of luck in the projects you undertake. Success can be yours if you use the concepts presented here.

Four Phases of Project Management

Phase I

➤ Determine objectives

➤ Select strategy

Phase II

➤ Write specifications

➤ Develop schedule

➤ Develop budget

Phase III

➤ Monitor performance

➤ Take corrective action

➤ Provide feedback

➤ Negotiate for materials, supplies, and services

➤ Resolve differences

Phase IV

➤ Deliver output

➤ Wrap up administrative details

➤ Evaluate the experience

PROJECT MANAGER'S CHECKLIST

❏ Define the project

❏ Select a strategy

❏ Develop specifications

❏ Develop a schedule

❏ Develop a budget

❏ Organize the project team

❏ Assign duties and responsibilities

❏ Train new team members

❏ Monitor progress

❏ Take corrective action

❏ Provide feedback

❏ Test final outcome

❏ Deliver outcome to client

❏ Write operations manual

❏ Train client personnel

❏ Reassign project staff

❏ Dispose of surplus equipment, materials, and supplies

❏ Release facilities

❏ Evaluate project performance

❏ Complete final audit

❏ Complete project report

❏ Review project with management

Project Management Software

Several good software packages are commercially available to help plan and monitor projects. Computers have made planning, modifying, contingency planning, and updating much easier, especially on large, complicated projects. But they still cannot define projects, set objectives, determine budgets or time requirements, or define control points, activities, or relationships. These very important activities must be done by a project manager and/or team members.

What to Expect from Project Planning Software

➤ Easy development of and changes to Gantt charts and PERT diagrams and calculation of the critical path.

➤ Easy production of schedules and budgets.

➤ Easy access to project information for preparing reports.

➤ Integration of project schedule with a calendar allowing for weekends and holidays.

➤ Easy access to different scenarios for contingency planning and updating.

➤ Easy checking for errors in logic and over-scheduling of individuals and groups.

Getting Started

When you work with project planning software for the first time, it is a good idea to experiment with it using a project you have already completed. This allows you to become familiar with the program before putting it to work.

Common Terms and Abbreviations in Project Management

ACWP	Actual Cost of Work Performed
B & P	Bid and Proposal
BAC	Budget at Completion
BCWP	Budgeted Cost of Work Performed
BCWS	Budgeted Cost of Work Scheduled
CCN	Contract Change Notice
CDR	Critical Design Review
CFE	Customer Furnished Equipment
CFSR	Contract Funds Status Report
CMO	Contract Management Office
CPFF	Cost Plus Fixed Fee
CPIF	Cost Plus Incentive Fee
CPM	Critical Path Method
C/SCSC	Cost/Schedule Control System Criteria
C/SSR	Cost/Schedule Status Report
EAC	Estimate at Completion
ETC	Estimate to Complete
FFP	Firm Fixed Price
FP	Fixed Price
G & A	General and Administrative
IR & D	Internal Research and Development
ODC	Other Direct Cost
PDR	Preliminary Design Review
PERT	Program Evaluation and Review Technique
PM	Project Manager or Management
PO	Purchase Order

PR	Purchase Requisition
RFP	Request for Proposal
RPQ	Request for Quotation
T & M	Time and Material
WBS	Work Breakdown Structure
WO	Work Order

Additional Reading

Cleland, David I. and Lewis R. Ireland. *Project Manager's Portable Guide.* NY: McGraw-Hill, 1999.

Forsberg, Kevin, Howard Cotterman, and Hal Mooz. *Visualizing Project Management.* NY: John Wiley & Sons, 2000.

Frame, J. Davidson. *Managing Projects in Organizations.* San Francisco: Jossey-Bass, Inc., 1995.

Haynes, Marion. *Effective Meeting Skills.* Menlo Park, CA: Crisp Publication, 1997.

Kerzner, Harold. *Project Management: A Systems Approach to Planning, Scheduling, and Controlling.* NY: John Wiley & Sons, 2000.

Kindler, Herb. *Managing Disagreement Constructively.* Menlo Park, CA: Crisp Publication, 1996.

Lambert, Lee R. and Erin Lambert. *Project Management: The CommonSense Approach.* Dublin, OH: Lambert Consulting Group, Inc., 2000.

Lewis, James P. *Mastering Project Management.* NY: McGraw-Hill, 1998.

Lewis, James P. *Project Planning, Scheduling, and Controlling.* NY: McGraw-Hill, 2000.

Maddox, Robert. *Successful Negotiation.* Menlo Park, CA: Crisp Publication, 1995.

Newbold, Robert C. *Project Management in the Fast Lane.* Winter Park, FL: Saint Lucie Press, 2000.

Pokras, Sandy. *Working in Teams.* Menlo Park, CA: Crisp Publication, 2002.

Williams, Paul B. *Getting a Project Done on Time.* NY: AMACON, 1996.

Wysocki, Robert K., David Beck, Jr., and David B. Crane. *Effective Project Management.* NY: John Wiley & Sons, 2000.

VERK

CRISP WORLDWIDE DISTRIBUTION

English language books are distributed worldwide. Major international distributors include:

ASIA/PACIFIC

Australia/New Zealand: In Learning, PO Box 1051, Springwood QLD, Brisbane, Australia 4127   Tel: 61-7-3-841-2286, Facsimile: 61-7-3-841-1580 ATTN: Messrs. Richard/Robert Gordon

Malaysia, Philippines, Singapore: Epsys Pte Ltd., 540 Sims Ave #04-01, Sims Avenue Centre, 387603, Singapore   Tel: 65-747-1964, Facsimile: 65-747-0162 ATTN: Mr. Jack Chin

Hong Kong/Mainland China: Crisp Learning Solutions, 18/F Honest Motors Building 9-11 Leighton Rd., Causeway Bay, Hong Kong   Tel: 852-2915-7119, Facsimile: 852-2865-2815 ATTN: Ms. Grace Lee

Japan: Phoenix Associates, Believe Mita Bldg., 8th Floor 3-43-16 Shiba, Minato-ku, Tokyo 105-0014, Japan   Tel: 81-3-5427-6231, Facsimile: 81-3-5427-6232 ATTN: Mr. Peter Owans

CANADA

Crisp Learning Canada, 60 Briarwood Avenue, Mississauga, ON L5G 3N6 Canada Tel: 905-274-5678, Facsimile: 905-278-2801 ATTN: Mr. Steve Connolly

EUROPEAN UNION

England: Flex Learning Media, Ltd., 9-15 Hitchin Street, Baldock, Hertfordshire, SG7 6AL, England Tel: 44-1-46-289-6000, Facsimile: 44-1-46-289-2417   ATTN: Mr. David Willetts

INDIA

Multi-Media HRD, Pvt. Ltd., National House, Floor 1 6 Tulloch Road, Appolo Bunder, Bombay, India 400-039 Tel: 91-22-204-2281, Facsimile: 91-22-283-6478 ATTN: Messrs. Ajay Aggarwal/ C.L. Aggarwal

SOUTH AMERICA

Mexico: Grupo Editorial Iberoamerica, Nebraska 199, Col. Napoles, 03810 Mexico, D.F. Tel: 525-523-0994, Facsimile: 525-543-1173   ATTN: Señor Nicholas Grepe

SOUTH AFRICA

Bookstores: Alternative Books, PO Box 1345, Ferndale 2160, South Africa Tel: 27-11-792-7730, Facsimile: 27-11-792-7787   ATTN: Mr. Vernon de Haas

Corporate: Learning Resources, P.O. Box 2806, Parklands, Johannesburg 2121, South Africa, Tel: 27-21-531-2923, Facsimile: 27-21-531-2944 ATTN: Mr. Ricky Robinson

MIDDLE EAST

Edutech Middle East, L.L.C., PO Box 52334, Dubai U.A.E. Tel: 971-4-359-1222, Facsimile: 971-4-359-6500   ATTN: Mr. A.S.F. Karim